THE MYSTIC

The Mystical Cosmos

JOSEPH MILNE

TEMENOS ACADEMY

THE TEMENOS ACADEMY
PATRON HRH THE PRINCE OF WALES

TEMENOS ACADEMY PAPERS NO. 37

These essays are based upon lectures
delivered to the Temenos Academy
at the Royal Asiatic Society, London
in March 2011

First published 2013 by
The Temenos Academy
16 Lincoln's Inn Fields
London WC2A 3ED

www.temenosacademy.org

Registered Charity no. 1043015

ISBN 978 0 9564078 9 4

Typeset by Agnesi Text, Hadleigh, Suffolk
Printed in the United Kingdom
at Smith Settle, Yeadon

The Temenos Academy wishes to thank Alexis Beddoe
for generously sponsoring the publication of this book

cover image
'Universal Man' illumination from
Hildegard's *Liber Divinorum Operum*, 1165
in public domain in European Union and Australia
see: http://en.wikipedia.org/wiki/
File:Hildegard von Bingen Liber Divinorum Operum.jpg

Dedicated to

DAVID CADMAN

for extraordinary kindness and encouragement

Contents

1

The Forgotten Metaphysics

⁓

IN THESE FOUR ESSAYS I shall attempt to draw our minds towards ways of thinking about the universe and reality which once existed but have since been overlaid by a different way of conceiving reality that emerged with the rationalism of the seventeenth century. As I have observed in previous lectures,[1] the manner in which a culture or an era conceives the cosmos reflects its fundamental way of being and its potential, in terms of possible knowledge, possible ethics and possible activity. And what determines the way the cosmos is conceived arises from a fundamental stance towards existence as such that each age adopts for itself. This stance precedes any model of reality, or any system of knowledge. Models and systems arise later, and are grounded in this primary orientation towards reality as such. So, for example, the modern scientific approach to cosmology presupposes that 'knowledge' of the universe is 'explanation' in calculative terms, in order that the coming into being and destiny of reality may be given adequate representation, or that an explanatory model may account for absolutely everything. Modern science, but especially modern physics, is said to be advancing in so far as it progresses towards that end.[2]

It is obvious that this contemporary idea of the meaning of knowledge is far from what Plato or Aristotle considered knowledge to be. For them knowledge of the cosmos was not for the sake of explanation or for accounting for everything in a single system or model. Their enquiries into reality are not a prelude to modern scientific

---

1 See Joseph Milne, *Metaphysics and the Cosmic Order* (Temenos Academy, 2008).
2 See Martin Héidegger, 'The Age of the World Picture' in *The Question Concerning Technology and Other Essays* (Harper and Row, 1977), for a detailed discussion of the underlying but hidden metaphysical presuppositions of the modern age.

enquiry as has often been claimed. Their concern for the truth of things is a fundamentally different kind of concern, and it therefore opens up an entirely different order of reality, an order completely passed over in the Age of Reason and the Enlightenment. For Plato and Aristotle the pursuit of truth is understood as adequate response to the Real, a coming into a right relationship with what most truly is. This is why for them the quest for knowledge is at once bound up with pure intellect and virtue. Without virtue real knowledge is not possible. There is a correlation between the quality of being in the knower and what is known. Thus knowledge of the truth of things cannot, for the ancient philosophers, be set down in a form which can be publicly disseminated. It cannot be detached from the communion with reality. It is more like the skill of the musician, where knowledge is active like a second nature in the act of playing, where the action is equal to the truth of the instrument and the music. Knowledge then becomes an obedience to reality. Because it arises from obedience to reality it requires intellectual and moral virtues.

The contrast I have drawn here between the Greek philosophers and modern scientific cosmology is not meant to dismiss modern science as such. What I wish to draw attention to is the difference in the underlying disposition towards reality in itself that distinguishes our age from that of classical Greece. What has happened is that the modern notion of knowledge, formulated as representational explanation, has taken up the empirical sciences in pursuit of knowledge conceived in that way. In short, a certain stance towards reality has come to be regarded as identical with scientific method. This is a mistake. But it is a mistake very hard to unravel because our culture no longer understands how to distinguish metaphysics from science, or the different modes of knowledge that belong to different orders of reality or being. Thus the claim of scientific fundamentalists that the scientific method is impartial and reliant exclusively on logical inference from evidence conceals within itself a presupposition about the nature of reality, and of the meaning of knowing, of which it is unaware and which it will not allow to be questioned. It is this unawareness of the real nature of this initial move towards reality and knowing that defines the contemporary relationship with the sciences, not the nature of the sciences as such. Indeed, scientific method was known and applied in classical Greece and throughout the Middle Ages, as has been well demonstrated by Pierre Duhem in his monumental *Medieval Cosmology*. But it was not then considered to lead to knowledge of the nature of reality.

It is the oblivion of different orders of knowledge that presents the greatest difficulty in understanding the contemporary conception of knowledge. The once obvious division between empirical, metaphysical and divine knowledge has been obliterated in the conflation of all enquiry into the empirical. Thus the very scope of what is to be known has been reduced, and the investment in the reductive method itself is determining what kind of knowledge may be sought.

What I would like to do in this first essay is give some sense of the nature of the profound difference between the manner of thinking of the ancients and modern thinking. To this end I would like to concentrate on just two aspects that belong to the approaches of Plato and Aristotle: namely the proper end of knowledge and the relation of human nature to reality or to the truth of things. In short, this is metaphysics. We shall find that these two aspects of ancient thought are continuously at play in Greek, Roman and Medieval thought or philosophy, and so they provide an illuminating way in to what we may now regard as a lost metaphysics.

First of all, then, the proper end of knowledge. As I suggested earlier, this involves a correlation between the knower and the known. Plato and Aristotle both express this fundamental position, although in different ways. For Plato the highest reality, that which is truly Real, may be known only by the highest intellect, in an act of pure contemplation in which the quality of the intelligence of the intellect corresponds with the quality of intelligence of the known, since, for Plato, only like may know like. For Aristotle, on the other hand, the human intellect or the mind is by nature oriented towards the truth of things. Just as the eye is oriented towards objects of light, or the ear to objects of sound, so likewise the mind is inclined towards and has an affinity with the truth of things.

All too often the positions of Plato and Aristotle have been reduced to systems and this has introduced a good deal of confusion. The most obvious example is the systematisation of Plato's Ideas, or Ideal Forms, into objects completely separate from the immediate presence of things. To speak of the 'world of the Ideas' is only an analogy, not a literal fact. So we have to be very cautious when we consider or speak of the distinction Plato draws between the appearances of things and the Ideas. The Ideas are, for Plato, the genuine actuality or real being of things, as distinct from their mode of appearing or their incidental qualities. Appearances and accidental qualities change, whilst the real actuality of a thing remains always the same and is grounded in its universal nature. It is this, the true actuality of things, which the intellect grasps and has affinity with, as distinct from what the senses discern. The senses do not discern the *being* of things, or that which makes a thing be itself, or its nature. These intelligible things belong to the intellect to know through its affinity with them. It is by virtue of this real truth of things that they then appear to the senses.

Aristotle's approach is rather different to Plato's, yet it belongs entirely to the Greek philosophical approach. For Aristotle the mind or soul is potentially all things. That is to say, that which is real of things conveys itself to the soul and becomes actual there. In this way the mind or soul is conformed to the truth of things, and through this knowing it becomes most actual itself. Which is, again, to say, when mind or intelligence moves from not knowing to knowing, it becomes more fully mind, because a mind without knowledge is only potential mind.

Aristotle also has been so systematised by subsequent philosophers and scholars that this initial act between mind and things has been rather lost, especially under the intricacies of logic. Logical inference only follows after the initial apprehension of things, while it is really this initial apprehension that is most mysterious and important to metaphysics. It is therefore worth noting that in the opening sentence of his *Metaphysics* Aristotle observes that all men by nature desire to know. Commenting on this assertion, Aquinas writes:

Three reasons can be given for this. The first is that each thing naturally desires its own perfection. Hence matter is also said to desire form as any imperfect thing desires its perfection. Therefore, since the intellect, by which man is what he is, considered in itself is all things potentially, and becomes them actually only through knowledge, because the intellect is none of the things that exists before it understands them, as stated in Book III of *The Soul* [429a23]; so each man naturally desires knowledge just as matter desires form.

The second reason is that each thing has a natural inclination to perform its proper operation . . . Now the proper operation of man as man is to understand, for by reason of this he differs from all other things.

The third reason is that it is desirable for each thing to be united to its source, since it is in this that the perfection of each thing consists . . . Now it is only by means of his intellect that man is united to the separate substances, which are the source of the human intellect and that to which the human intellect is related as something imperfect to something perfect. It is for this reason, too, that the ultimate happiness of man consists in this union. Therefore man naturally desires to know.[3]

From the ancient Greek philosophers to Aquinas in the late Middle Ages it was understood that a relation existed between the human mind and the nature of things. In this respect there is no real difference between Plato's understanding that only like can know like and Aristotle's understanding that the intellect is only perfected in uniting with its source in the substance of things.

In light of this, there is an interesting passage in Aristotle's *Physics* in which he remarks how the ancient philosophers, in seeking to explain the origins of things according to which element came first, failed to observe the first thing about things, which is their *ousia* or

---

3 Thomas Aquinas, *Commentary on Aristotle's Metaphysics*, trans. John P. Rowan (Dumb Ox Books, 1995).

'beingness'. The Greek *ousia* is usually translated as 'substance', from 'substantia' in Latin. But the modern use of 'substance' does not quite carry the original meaning. We get nearer to that meaning in the word 'substantial' in the sense of 'ample'. What Aristotle is pointing out by using the word *ousia* is that the Pre-Socratic philosophers, in their speculations on the origin of things, passed over the one thing that brought things to their minds in the first place, their presentness, their very being there in their act of being.[4]

This beingness or presentness of things is not like our modern notion of 'fact'. The facts of thing are secondary and often transitory. What Aristotle is observing is that what first presents itself to the intelligence is Being, not features or characteristics or qualities, and that all else that might be known of things follows only after Being. More than this, it is the being of things that is communicative, and which most corresponds with the mind that apprehends. Thus when mind apprehends being it at once comes into knowledge of its own being, or becomes self-reflective.

Just as Plato's theory of Ideas has become distorted through systematisation, so likewise has Aristotle's attention to the *ousia* of things similarly become distorted. It has long been claimed that Aristotle was an empiricist, in contrast to Plato who was an idealist. Both these categorisations are distortions and lead us away from the real ways of thinking of these Greek philosophers. Ironically, those who claim Aristotle as an empiricist make exactly the same mistake as those Pre-Socratic philosophers he called into question for passing over *ousia*, the beingness or presentness of things. By saying this Aristotle is not an empiricist, rather he is making the ontological observation that it is the being of things that first presents itself to the mind, and that this is immediately the very subtlest thing that can present itself to the intelligence.

Thus where Plato and Aristotle clearly agree is that the truth of things is that which is the most real or actual of things. Truth and

---

4 See Aristotle, *Metaphysics* Book Zeta. The best translation, which deals with the special problems of Aristotle's terminology, is *Aristotle's Metaphysics*, trans. Joe Sachs (Green Lion Press, 2002).

actuality almost amount to the same thing in their philosophy, and are regarded as that which it is proper to the intellect to know. Truth is therefore not an abstraction from things, a rational representation of them. On the contrary, it is what most belongs to things in so far as they are real or are in being. It is their own, their actuality as possessed by themselves. Yet it is also what is most communicable of things. For Plato it is what is embodied in all appearances, that which shines in any coming to be. For Aristotle it is the immediate being-ness of things. Truth is at once the real and the disclosure of the real, since everything is by nature self-revealing or self-manifesting, and not merely as expression but as disclosing towards everything. All real things are in communion with one another in their truth.

It is at this point that we arrive at one of the most interesting and extraordinary insights of Greek thought: all things are oriented towards being known. Reality is not the mere passive object of the human desire to know and understand, but rather the correlate of the potential of the mind to know. Human knowing is determined by the reality and being of things to communicate themselves. Thus the very subtlest knowledge of things is conferred upon the human intelligence as a gift given by truth itself.

It is within this reciprocal epistemology that we can discern in principle what it is proper for the human mind to know and how it is proper to things to be known. In both Plato and Aristotle things are oriented towards being known, and their relation to the reciprocity of the mind is part of their nature, just as the relation of the mind to things is part of its nature. To 'be known' belongs to their nature in the same way as it belongs to them 'to be'.

There is a profound reason for this connaturality between the truth or being of things and the mind. It follows from the principle that what is most real, or most fully actual, is of the highest and most self-sufficient order of things. For Plato and Platonism subsequently this is ultimately the One Itself, which stands above every order of being and as the source of all that is. That which comes into being from the One emanates in descending order, from the highest and most autonomous powers down to the lowest and least autonomous. For

Aristotle, who comes at it in his different manner, all things may be traced back until we arrive at the principle that brings all things into being and orders their actions or functions throughout the cosmos – this is the Unmoved Mover. In either case the First Principle is at once the highest, most actual and eternal, and that upon which all else depends and derives its being and function.

This way of understanding things is paralleled by the gods, who likewise order the cosmos according to the highest and most intellectual principles and thus sustain all things in being. I am not saying that the metaphysical view and the theistic are exactly identical with one another. The poets and the philosophers see and think in their own ways. But what is clear is that in either way of articulating the order of things, the highest and most autonomous or self-determining comes first, and that all things are manifestations in their own natures of this most primordial actuality. The cosmos in principle comes into being downwards from the highest, and because of this the things that belong to the realm of generation – the living kingdom – incline in their growth towards the principle they come from, that is, they inherently seek to be as fully actual as their nature has the potential to become. Hence the acorn seeks to become the oak. Or as Plato puts it in the *Timaeus*, all things strive towards the perfection they derive from, the lower realms imitating so far as they can the motions of the higher realms.

This brings us to our second theme, the relation of human nature to reality or truth. The clue to this lies in what we have already seen of the correspondence between the human mind and the truth of things. On the one hand, the mind is ordained towards the truth of things, as its natural operation, while on the other hand the truth of things is ordained towards being known. As Plato says in the *Timaeus*, the soul is brought to its own proper order and harmony through contemplating the heavens, because the cosmic motions are rational and unperturbed, which is also the natural state of the human intellect. The harmonious order of 'Nature in itself' is rational and unerring and thus the natural object of intellectual contemplation, in which

Nature finds a likeness of itself. So the first characteristic of the relation of human nature to the truth of things is that the truth of things brings human nature into 'harmony and agreement with itself' as Plato puts it.[5] When human nature is in harmony with itself, it is at the same moment in agreement and harmony with the intelligent order of the universe. It then lives and acts according to its own law and nature. Yet in order to attain this inner harmony the intelligence must be receptive of the outer harmony of the universe. Here is where Aristotle's understanding of the mind throws light, in that in his understanding the soul is potentially all things, in the sense of being infinitely open and receptive to the truth that things communicate of themselves to the intelligence.

Because the intellect has this capacity to receive the knowledge imparted to it by the communicative power of things themselves, it also has the capacity to discern the unity of all things. At one level it discerns this unity as the awe-inspiring order among all the parts of Nature, where each part at once tends to its own particular perfection and to the universal perfection of all beings. At another level it discerns the principle of unity itself, the eternal, unchanging unity upon which the infinitely various unity of Nature depends and evolves. Through this receptivity the intellect is able to comprehend the One and the Many in agreement with one another, and Motion and Rest in agreement with one another, because these are resolved in the intelligible truth of things known in their essential reality.

When Socrates says that philosophy begins in wonder he means the natural attraction of the mind to this underlying intelligible order that binds all things to a single end. This wonder of itself already tempers the mind and draws the human faculties to their proper functions. There are certain things which can only be seen when the mind is in a state of wonder. This quite simple fact of human nature which everyone knows is a key to the relation between knowledge and virtue. We noted earlier that for Plato and Aristotle knowledge of the truth of things is possible only for the virtuous person. The

---

5 See especially *Timaeus* 47.

immediate reason for this is quite simple: only a person able to act according to the truth of things will have the capacity to contemplate truth. This is why the first virtue in Greek ethics is prudence, which is the capacity to rightly discern things. The virtues are the qualities of being that gather together the faculties of the soul and make it master of itself and so keep it free from the tyranny of transitory desires and passions which arise through the misperception of things and thereby establishing wrong relations with them. Seen from this point of view, vice is simply response or action that is out of accord with the real nature of things.

Modern theories of knowledge do not generally see any connection between virtue and the capacity to know. Modern ethical theories are in great confusion because of this.[6] But for the Greek philosophers and the Medieval scholars the intellect and the conscience were always connected. In Plato the questions raised in the dialogues about the nature of things always have an ethical context, and often also a sacred context. In the *Republic* the various methods that are explored concerning statecraft, education or the arts always have an ethical purpose in mind. The ideal statesman is the most just man. The purpose of education of the young is to develop outward and inner strength in order that they may fully partake in the general good of society. All the enquiries undertaken in the *Republic* belong to the realm of justice. And the concern of justice is how to bring the human realm into harmony with the universal order.

In Plato's *Laws* the relation between virtue and knowledge is yet more explicit, and in a sense this is why this particular dialogue seems the most distant from the thinking of our own age. The question is raised: If we were to found a new city state, how would we go about formulating its laws? This is the longest of Plato's dialogues and we have to pass through several books before we even begin to get any kind of practical answer. The reason for this is simple: only those of

6 For a full discussion of the modern problems of ethical understanding see Alasdair MacIntyre *Whose Justice? Which Rationality?* (University of Notre Dame Press, 1988).

sufficient wisdom and courage would be able to discern good laws and be able to abide by them. This combination of wisdom and virtue is precisely the connection between reason and ethics, between intellect and conscience. The explanation for this necessary connection is again quite simple. The wise who lack courage will not be able to hold constantly to what is right or truthful. They need also to be courageous for their wisdom to be constant and effective. On the other hand, the courageous who lack wisdom will apply their courage rashly and foolishly, perhaps throwing away their lives needlessly. So courage must be informed by reason and wisdom for it to be able to serve the common good and the truth of things. The greater part of the *Laws* is concerned with the preconditions of human character that are required if good laws are to be formulated. It is clear that if such a city state were attempted by those lacking in wisdom or courage they would never be able to know which laws to formulate, and so it would fail, either through the slackness of the wise who lack courage, or through the tyranny of the courageous who lack wisdom.[7]

We also find that the same concern for virtue underlies the *Timaeus*. In this dialogue we have Plato's famous cosmological myth, which has been profoundly influential throughout western thought and especially in the Middle Ages. It is easy to lift the long speech of Timaeus on the cosmos from the context of the dialogue. It then appears to read as an explanation of the creation of the universe – a cosmology in the modern scientific sense, but expressed as a myth. But the real context of it springs from the question of how Athens was originally founded and how its first laws were instituted, laws which ultimately derive from Athena who combines in her nature wisdom and courage, the two qualities required for the founding of any city state that is likely to endure. Plato's enquiry into cosmology is rooted in the question of how we ought to live, and what are the universal laws which govern human society.[8]

---

7 See especially *Laws* Books I–III.
8 See the excellent Introduction to *Plato's Timaeus*, trans. Peter Kalkavage (Focus Publishing, 2001).

From these examples we can begin to grasp how it was for the Greek philosophers that the proper end of the intellect can be accomplished only when virtue is present. Only when the intelligence is informed by wisdom and tempered by virtue does it have the capacity to align itself in accord with the truth manifest in things. Only then is human nature really connected with reality and at the same time ordered inwardly according to its own proper nature.

There is a further reason why knowledge and virtue belong together. All things ultimately seek the Good, and for Plato in particular the Good and the Truth are the same. For Aristotle the universal good manifests in the way every part of Nature seeks to actualize its own perfection and at the same time serve the good of the whole. Each thing attains its perfection first in fully coming into being according to its proper nature, and secondly through its *act* within the whole of Nature. For every particular thing that comes into being its nature is partly determined by its place and function within the whole. Nothing can come properly into being if it does not serve the whole, simply because each thing is born out of the whole. For Plato the unity of all the parts of the cosmos come closest to the perfection that the manifest order may have to the absolute perfection of the One Itself that all things seek to imitate as their good. For Aristotle the unity of the whole cosmos is the principle that gives to each particular part its essential character and place within the unity. Thus unity and diversity mutually embody and sustain each other. But the relation of the part to the whole is not merely a mechanistic relation, like the unity of parts in a geometric pattern. Rather it is an active relation, an extension of the act of particular being outwardly towards the universal being. This Aristotelian understanding of act is really very important and we shall return to it later. But for now it is very helpful to keep in mind that for Aristotle the understanding of being does not stop simply at the coming into being of things in their particular being, but continues into the act each being performs within the totality of reality, and how through its act it extends itself to the universal good and acts for the being of all beings. In this sense, then, Nature herself is virtuous and continually strives to bring together in her acts a complete unity between being, knowledge and goodness.[9]

In this regard, then, human virtue as a prerequisite for the knowledge of truth is an extension of a principle already found in Nature, even at the least intelligible levels. The substantial difference between the human level and the other less autonomous levels is that human nature may extend to embrace and participate in the whole of reality. Human nature is distinguished as being potentially receptive to all knowledge. But this also means that human nature is responsible to all things. In terms of the whole, it is not in accord with human nature to act in unwitting ignorance of the truth of things.

Nothing is more ancient or more primordial in philosophic and religious history than the sense that every human act stands in judgement before the court of reality as a whole. The Old Testament in particular often expresses this very intensely, while in the Greek philosophers there remains always the question of how to appease Fate. In one way this situation leads to the difficult questions of theodicy, while in another it opens the way to grasp the depth of man's ethical relation to reality. The Greek response to this was to come to understand that human nature cannot be irresponsible even towards itself, and that particular being is responsible to Being as a whole. It is this insight which animates the philosophy of Plato and Aristotle, over and above any differences between them. Knowledge, being and goodness belong completely together, both in the cosmos as a whole and in human nature in particular.

For Plato as well as for Aristotle, then, knowledge is understood as a mode of participation in the truth of things. It is not representative descriptions of reality but rather an act of being receptive and responsive to reality. For this reason it is also ethical, since such receptivity and responsiveness is possible only when the human constitution and character are in harmony, and this inner harmony is

9 This Greek understanding of Nature as oriented towards the good played a central role in Medieval theology. See Oliva Blanchette, *The Perfection of the Universe According to Aquinas: A Teleological Cosmology* (Pennsylvania State University Press, 1992) for a detailed study.

virtue. For these great Greek philosophers the truth of things and the goodness of things cannot be separated, and so the desire to know the truth is as much the desire to know the good. But also the capacity to know the cosmos is bound up with the capacity to know human nature. So for Aristotle the object of studying ethics is not in order to become virtuous, since he assumes his readers are already virtuous, but rather in order to understand one's own nature and to become self-reflective, to become conscious of the real nature of action in action. Thus the capacity for outer and inner knowledge are bound together. And the purpose of all knowing is for the sake of coming into accord with the truth of things, in both thought and action. For Plato and Aristotle this accord with the truth of things is the only way that the good and the happy life may be attained.

We need hardly draw attention to the contrast between this ancient way of thought and that of our own times. It is perhaps the loss of this connection between the true and the good that distinguishes modernity from the classical understanding of reality or of Nature. Nor is it as simple as a difference between Greek cosmology and modern cosmology. The real difference lies at the philosophical or metaphysical level, and in particular in what is held to be the proper purpose of knowledge.

For the modern age the purpose of knowledge has been taken to be either mastery over Nature, or theoretical explanation of Nature. Neither of these ends are accounted proper ends in Greek philo-sophy – not because they are necessarily bad or even unattainable, but because they do not accord with the proper end of human nature, which is attained through thinking and acting in accord with the truth of things. This difference between modern and ancient under-standing of the purpose of knowledge is entirely a metaphysical difference. It is a really important difference, because often it is assumed that it is the scientific method itself that divides our age from that of the ancients. It would be more accurate to say that the modern age has assumed that the scientific method can respond to metaphysical and ethical questions, while clearly it cannot. It is in the reduction of the orders of knowledge to the scientific method alone that the essential difference lies. It is worth seeing how Descartes proposes his new method which became the basis of the modern approach to the question of reality:

> So soon as I had acquired some general notions concerning Physics . . . they caused me to see that it is possible to attain knowledge which is very useful in life, and that, instead of that speculative philosophy which is found in the Schools, we may find a practical philosophy by means of which, knowing the force and the action of fire, water, air, the stars, heaven, and all the other bodies that environ us, as distinctly as we know the different crafts of our artisans, we can in the same way employ them in all those uses to which they are adapted, and thus render ourselves as the masters and possessors of nature.[10]

Because of this exclusive commitment to one approach it follows that the great questions of ontology and epistemology no longer have a place within the scheme of truth-knowing. It is surely an extraordinary thing that the realms of knowledge that were once considered to be the most essential have now become peripheral, or even largely incomprehensible. But this is an inevitable consequence of the reductive approach to knowledge. In effect it reduces the world itself down to one realm or one dimension.

In the essays that follow I will try to show how this great loss might be recovered, not by dismissing the sciences, but through reconnecting with the realms of knowledge now obscured or discounted. I hope to show that through adopting a different stance towards the truth of things, what may be seen changes. And I hope to show that only through such a change of bearing towards things can the truly philosophical manner of knowing take place, and from that a reli-

---

10 René Descartes, *Discourse on the Method*, in *The Philosophical Works of Descartes, Volume 1*, ed. Elizabeth S. Haldane and G. R. T. Ross (Cambridge University Press, 1980), p. 119.

gious manner of knowing may be possible in which the created world may be understood as the manifestation or mystical revelation of God.

2

The Ancient View of Nature

⌒

WE OBSERVED IN THE PREVIOUS ESSAY that for Plato and Aristotle there is an ethical dimension to knowledge, because knowledge of the truth of things involves a correspondence between the integrity of human nature and the order of Nature. This ethical comportment towards the truth of things, which makes it possible for them to be known, is not only fundamental but it also corresponds with other concerns with the nature of reality which are equally essential. In seeking to understand Nature the intellect is searching out what is permanent, what is fully actual and what is good. These are the things that concern the philosophical enquiry into Nature that characterise Plato and Aristotle, and which distinguish their enquiry from the contemporary scientific enquiry into Nature.

While these characteristics are made explicit in Plato and Aristotle, they may be traced back as far as recorded literature will allow. The most ancient literature expresses these features symbolically or mythically. As Eliade observes,

> the perspective of religious man of the archaic societies is that the world exists because it was created by the gods, and that the existence of the world itself 'means' something, 'wants to say' something, that the world is neither mute nor opaque, that it is not an inert thing without purpose or significance. For religious man, the cosmos 'lives' and 'speaks'.[1]

This 'signifying' or 'speaking' power of the world is a property that links the religious and the philosophical approach towards the truth

---

1 Mircea Eliade, *The Sacred and the Profane* (Harcourt Brace Jovanovich, 1959), p. 165.

of things. The world is not merely passively 'there' but actively revealing something through being there and manifesting itself, and it is this that man is called to know and to engage with. Without such engagement one is not really human, as Plato suggests in *Gorgias*:

> And philosophers tell us that communion and friendship and orderliness and temperance and justice bind together heaven and earth and gods and men, and that the universe is therefore called Cosmos or order, not disorder or misrule.[2]

We observe here that the qualities that distinguish the virtuous human nature are those also of the universe. Communion and friendship, orderliness, temperance and justice, these are the qualities of the virtuous person. Communion refers to the capacity to participate to the fullest extent in the wholeness of reality, friendship refers to the loyalty and honour in which only the virtuous can share. Orderliness and temperance refer to the proportionate and rational harmony of the being, within and without, while justice emerges as the universal principle which governs all things in their proper relations and functions. Thus justice 'binds together heaven and earth and gods and men', which means that the universal order and the particular order reciprocate one another, and that the divine knowledge of the gods guides the life of men, while the virtuous actions of men delight the gods. It is this correlation between the different levels of reality which demonstrates that the universe is a Cosmos, 'not disorder or misrule'.

These are the things that make the universe a cosmos, and so for Plato the opposite of cosmos is misrule or injustice. The word 'cosmos' in Greek is etymologically connected with the word '*dike*', justice, and it is clear that for Plato and Aristotle the idea of order or cosmos means justice between all things, not merely some mechanical order without any ethical dimension. It is worth noting that in our times the words 'universe' and 'cosmos' no longer have any ethical

2 Plato, *Gorgias* 507–508.

meaning, but at best refer to mechanistic laws.[3] So the notion that the universe could be virtuous is very strange to the modern conception of reality, and yet this view remained central to western philosophy and Christianity until the close of the Middle Ages. We find it in St Augustine and Boethius, and also in Dante's *De Monarchia* where he says:

> Every son is in a good (indeed, ideal) state when he follows in the footsteps of a perfect father, insofar as his nature allows. Mankind is the son of heaven, which is quite perfect in all its workings; for man and the sun generates man, as we read in the second book of the *Physics*. Therefore mankind is in an ideal state when it follows the footsteps of [the skies], insofar as its nature allows. And, since the whole sphere of [the skies] is guided by a single movement . . . and by a single source of motion . . , then . . . mankind is in an ideal state when it is guided by a single ruler (as by a single source of motion) and in accordance with a single law (as by a single movement).[4]

This correlation between human virtue and cosmic perfection and justice, although universal in all ancient cosmologies, takes two different forms. One form is that of ritual propitiation of Nature or the gods. Through sacrificial action the order of the heavens is maintained and human society flourishes. This ritual propitiation has been long discounted in modern thought as animism or primitivism. According to this view human sacrificial actions have no effect upon the indifferent forces of Nature.

We can find instances of this first form in Plato, but predominantly Plato represents the second form. Here the roles are reversed and the

---

3 See David L. Schindler, ed., *Beyond Mechanism* (University Press of America, 1986), for a discussion of the problems encountered in relating the religious approach to the universe with that of quantum physics, with two contributions by David Bohm.

4 Quoted in Remi Brague, *The Wisdom of the World* (University of Chicago Press, 2004), p. 140.

human realm is brought into conformity with the universe. Thus the justice that animates the heavens and which remains always constant becomes the model for human justice and for the foundation of society. It is this understanding that underlies the plans of many ancient cities based upon the configuration of the heavens, and which still remains even today in the orientation of churches and especially in the great cathedrals.[5]

So when I suggest that the manner in which an age conceives the universe determines the way society lives and the ends it pursues, this really is true and always revealing. Any age or any culture will have a notion of how it is 'situated' in the overall scheme of reality, and it will act according to that notion in its arts, education, law, religion and ethics.

One way in particular in which this can be seen is in the difference between the ancient Greek understanding of space and that of the modern age. We need to be alert to this difference because we can seriously misunderstand Plato and Aristotle if we are not. For Plato and Aristotle, and of course ancient Greek understanding generally, space is understood as belonging to things and as their abiding place. Each thing has its space in the universe, its place of being where it dwells. Thus it is the abiding of each thing that creates the space for that thing, just as it is a human being that creates a house to dwell in. Space is not an emptiness into which things are thrown, as in Newtonian space.[6]

This ancient understanding of space is linked to another property of things which also has been displaced by the Newtonian space. Each thing in nature has its own motion. Again for Plato and Aristotle 'motion' does not mean mere abstract movement, it means the

---

5 For a fascinating study of the city in the Middle Ages and its relation to the cosmos and the body of Christ see Keith Lilley, *City and Cosmos: The Medieval World in Urban Form* (Reaktion Books, 2009).

6 For an incisive discussion of the essential differences between the classical Greek understanding of nature and Newtonian science see the essay by Martin Heidegger 'Modern Science, Metaphysics, and Mathematics' in *Basic Writings* (Routledge, 1996), p. 271 ff.

autonomy of each natural thing. The motion of a thing is the way it moves itself, and this includes the form it takes in its coming to be and its end in relation to all Nature. In contrast to this, the modern conception of motion is founded on the idea that things are moved from outside themselves, and that if they were not compelled to move they would cease to move altogether. For the Greek philosophers all living things are understood as self-moving, as autonomous, while yet participating in the whole. Thus the tree or the horse have their own motions which belongs to their nature. They do not merely exist as the outcome of causes or conditions outside themselves. From within themselves they seek the perfection and fullness of being that belongs to their nature, and in this way they participate in the universal justice of Nature as a whole.

So space as dwelling place brought into being by each being, and the power of self-motion or autonomy that belongs to each being are two components which make up the 'being there' of each being. In other words, the Greek notion of space is a metaphysical understanding which *sees* ontologically, that is to say, which looks upon things according to their manner of being. By contrast the modern idea of space has removed the ontological dimension and replaced it with the merely measurable or quantitative. This is what William Blake refers to as Newton's sleep, the reduction of reality to a single dimension. In Book IV of *Physics* Aristotle considers and rejects the notion of space as empty extension and dismisses it as a misuse of mathematical imagination, a false relation of theory to reality or being.

This ancient understanding of space and motion throws further light on the passage in the *Timaeus* which directs the soul to conform itself with the intelligent motions of the heavens. The universal order and the coming to be of the universe is as just and as perfect as it can be, and since the human soul is oriented towards the truth of things, it comes into agreement with itself through coming into harmony with the universal order. Plato means that the human intelligence comes to itself through the likeness of itself in the manner of being and dwelling of the universe – its motion and space. And since this relation is ontological at the level of intellect, it also means that the individual being comes into its proper relation with Being as such. This is the 'communion and friendship' that Plato speaks of in the *Gorgias* in which human nature becomes most fully itself through its receptivity to the just and temperate order of the universe. And since at the intelligible level all things participate in all things, the work of man as philosopher is to bring into conscious reflection this given-ness of the natural order. For Aristotle this conscious reflection is contemplation, or *theoria*, which is the proper end of the intellectual understanding.[7]

These considerations of motion and space lead us to the question of causality, to which Aristotle gives careful attention. From what we have said so far Aristotle's understanding of causality cannot be identical to our modern notion of causality, which regards things that come to be as the effects of things prior to them, either as materially or historically prior. The reason this view cannot be correct is because for Aristotle things belong to themselves, or arise into being out of their own nature, are self-moving and are part of the entire order of the universe. Therefore anything that comes into being cannot be merely an effect or subsidiary to a cause materially or historically prior to itself. In a way, to regard things as merely the effects of prior causes is to deprive them of their own mode of being and belonging in the order of things, or to subsume them into some secondary being.

Aristotle's answer to the question of causality is therefore onto-logical. It asks, what is the manner of coming to be of things? For example, what is the manner of coming to be of a tree? Looked at in this way the coming to be of the tree is part of the act of being of the tree, its *energeia* or being-at-work. This coming to be of the tree, and abiding in being, and dwelling in its place of being, all belong to the actuality of the tree, and arise from its potential which belongs to its Form. To put it another way, the tree comes to be because its nature is

---

7 For contemplation as the proper end of understanding see Aristotle, *Nicomachean Ethics* Book 10.

to abide in being and to be-at-work in being. This being-at-work in being includes the end or *telos* of the tree, that is to say its completeness in its own particular mode of being, or what is called its final cause.

In his notes on his translation of Aristotle's *Physics* Joe Sachs writes:

> The two ultimate ideas that govern Aristotle's thinking are *thinghood* (*ousia*) and *being-at-work* (*energeia*).
>
> The primary fact about the world we experience is that it consists of independent things (*ouiai*), each of which is a *this* (*tode ti*), an enduring whole, and *separate* (*choriston*), or intact. Since thinghood is characterised by *wholeness* (*to telos*), the wholeness of each independent thing has the character of an *end* (*telos*), or *that for the sake of which* (*hou heneka*) it does all that it does. This doing is therefore the being-at-work that makes it what it is, since it is *what it keeps on being in order to be at all* (*to ti einai*). Thus thinghood and being-at-work merge into the single idea of *being-at-work-staying-itself* (*entelecheia*).[8]

We could say a great deal more about causality here, but I wish to draw attention in particular to the contrast between Aristotle's meaning of causality and our modern notion. The two forms in which modern causality are conceived, as material cause or historical cause, result in the object explained getting replaced by something prior to itself. This is the case in both modern materialism and intelligent design theory – whether the prior cause is matter or an intelligent designer logically makes no difference because both theories arise from the same way of thinking, and both reduce the being of things to an effect of something other. It is for this reason that Aristotle rejects the materialist explanation. It takes things for less than they are. Aristotle invites us to look at the act of being present of things, which means we must be present along with them, in the act of seeing

---

8 *Aristotle's Physics: A Guided Study*, trans. Joe Sachs (Rutgers University Press, 2008), p. 31.

and knowing. It is this knowledge that communicates itself from things to the intelligence. For Aristotle things do not need to be displaced by theories or formulas in order to be known or understood. That is the danger of the mathematician who takes an undynamic mathematical formula and attempts to reduce the presence of things to that formula. This is what Descartes does in taking empty space geometry as the ideal model for knowledge of the objective world. For Aristotle mere quantitative mathematics is a static science and therefore cannot correlate to the dynamic abiding in being of things, or that for which they come into being. In other words, it cannot deal with ontology in all its aspects.

For Aristotle the sensible and the intelligible are present together, and the appearing of things and the intelligible cannot be separated, although they are each distinct. This idea seems strange to our modern way of thinking where it is assumed that if we can grasp the laws or mechanisms of things we have more knowledge of them than they are in themselves, especially where such knowledge may be mathematically formulated. This way of thinking is not confined to modern physics but extends to economics, banking, sociology, to anything that can be turned into calculation or computation. Because this approach does correlate with an aspect of things, it gets taken as more true and more knowable than the things themselves. In part it is taken as more true than the things themselves because number seems more certain than any other kind of model of things, as Descartes asserts, and so *that* certainty is erroneously carried over to displace things themselves. But this calculated representation is also taken as more true than things themselves because it is an intelligible abstraction that has a kind of endurance beyond the things themselves. Thus, according to this way of thinking, Stephen Hawking claims that the latest theory of physics makes religion and philosophy redundant. His claim is logical given his regard for modern mathematics as ideal representation, but illogical in so far as the mathematical cannot account for the philosophical or the religious. Hawking is making the false assumption that because the mathematical cannot account for the philosophical and the religious realms of knowledge on their own terms, they therefore refer to the nonexistent, or are superfluous to real knowledge. That there could be different orders of reality and different modes of knowledge belonging to them seems inconceivable to this kind of reductive science.

What is important to note here is that the modern resort to the mathematical separates the sensible from the intelligible, and that Aristotle was aware of this danger in thinking. Thus he dismisses various theories of Nature which separate the sensible from the intelligible in coming to his more comprehensive view, in which the presence of things and the knowing of things remain bound together and reciprocal. Thus speculative theories cannot displace things. And what holds knowledge and things together for Aristotle is his fundamental question that asks *what it means to be*. This is the question of his *Physics*.

The word translated as 'nature' is the Greek '*phusis*' from which we derive our modern word 'physics'. But neither the modern word *nature* nor the word *physics* have the meaning they have for Aristotle. For him *phusis* means the activity of all things as 'seen in their birth, growth, and self-maintenance and independence of things and the equilibrium of the parts of the cosmos'.[9] Essentially it means the activity of being, the manner in which things come to be, grow, perfect themselves and relate to the act of being of the whole cosmos. We have to remember that the word 'being' is a verb, and that Aristotle is concerned to understand Nature as in *act* or as underway, seeking the fullness of being. So the kind of seeing or understanding of nature that Aristotle is concerned with is to observe *that for which* all the activity of being is occurring, the *telos* of things.

Once again it is worth drawing attention to the contrast between Aristotle's concern for the coming to be of things and the modern mathematical account of things. The mathematical account of things pays no regard to the end for which things come to be. This is not to say that our age cannot observe things coming to be and taking their place in the order of Nature as a whole, but modern thought does not

9 Sachs, *Aristotle's Physics*, p. 31.

regard this as of fundamental concern. This is because the question of that for which the universe has come to be seems an impossible question for modern man. And the question of that for which human life has come to be seems an equally impossible question.[10] But these two questions, which really belong together and for Plato and Aristotle are never separated, seem impossible questions to modern man only because the prevailing epistemology cannot accommodate such questions, because they lie outside the model of what counts as knowledge. No proffered *answer* would fit the prevailing model of reality.

It is this teleological order of Nature that presents great difficulty. There is a history of how this aspect of Nature was lost. Once the idea of space changed from being the natural abiding place of each thing and became a mere emptiness in which things were pushed from one position to another, the understanding of things as self-moving was lost. And once the autonomy of things was lost, the communion of things was lost, and so the universe gradually became seen as filled with separate entities being shifted from one position to another.

Many years ago in my teens when I first began to read philosophers I came upon a passage in Bertrand Russell which said 'industry is nothing else than moving things from one place to another'. I was shocked, but did not appreciate then that modern philosophy, or at least logical positivism, was dedicated to this kind of reductionism. This example is interesting, though, because it shows how a description of things which is true in a completely mechanistic sense, void of any intelligence or purpose, entirely misses the actual nature of the thing being defined. This kind of stripping down to the least ontological aspect of things is precisely opposite to the approach of Aristotle or of Plato.

There is a different type of *reductio*, as the scholastics called it, which traces the order of things to the *highest* and most complete

---

10 These questions elude even the most serious ecological investigations, even though we experience deep disquiet over how Nature is conceived in modern science.

principles.[11] This is the reverse of what Russell tries to do in his logical positivism. In his *Physics* Aristotle seeks to understand Nature according to the subtlest and most comprehensive principle, the being of being or the meaning of being, and this means tracing things to the highest and most intelligent principle. This highest and most intelligent principle is not an abstract notion, or a mere explanatory representation, but rather the fullness of the presence of things in their act of abiding. This order of the truth of things is where the fullest correspondence between the intellect and things is found, since it is this intelligible act of abiding that is communicable from things to the mind. For Aristotle it is the *first known* but *last understood*. That is to say, it is always what is immediately apprehended, yet only through the rational process of philosophical reflection can it be understood.

This brings us to the very delicate question of the relation of thought to the being of things. At the beginning of this essay I said that in seeking to understand Nature the intellect is searching out what is permanent, what is fully actual and what is good. Here is where Plato and Aristotle are in complete accord. However, in the history of Western thought the understanding of the relationship between the immediate presence of things and the eternal, the fully actual and the good has shifted around considerably. In general there has been a drift to separate these highest realities from the immediate being of things, and this tendency is to be found in the Neo-Platonists as much as in the Christian theologians.

In short, the highest things have tended to be moved to a transcendental realm and the lower things to a mortal realm. Corresponding with this tendency has grown up a separation of thought from the things thought upon. By this I mean that it becomes questionable whether there is any real relation between things in themselves and the discernment of their principles and attributes. Is our thought of things actually grounded in things, or is it only a construction of the mind? Likewise, are the universal qualities we

---

11 A classic work of this kind is Bonaventure's *De Reductione Artium ad Theologiam*, trans. Sister Emma Therese Healy (The Franciscan Institute, 1951).

discern in things, such as beauty or truth, actually present in each instance or are these abstractions that exist only in thought?

These connected questions have also been raised time and again throughout Western thought, and all the variants of idealism, realism, dualism, materialism, creationism, emanationism, phenomenology, nominalism and so on have arisen from the responses to these questions. This is a notoriously complex area, so it is not uncommon for one thinker to be claimed by several of these different schools of thought. For example Plato is often regarded as a radical dualist, but also as a radical monist, while Aristotle has been regarded as an anti-Platonic materialist but also as the supreme abstract logician. It takes a lot of meticulous work to avoid projecting these notions back upon the ancient philosophers.

So the question remains as to the real relation between things and thought, and between things and their universal principles. I wish to propose that for both Plato and Aristotle the relation of things to thought is a real ontological relation, and that the relation of things to principles is also a real ontological relation. To put that quite simply, thought receives the real from things just as the senses do in their kind. And also that the universal principles of things are what most belong to them in their actuality. For example, each of us present now is a human being, and this is known by each of us in a way that makes possible the highest kind of discourse and knowing, because that is what essentially makes us human beings. There is no difficulty with the fact that we are made up of different aspects, such as matter, mind, histories, virtues and so on. All these things are embraced as a unity, and it is only when embraced as a unity that we know a person as a person.

My point is that there is no problem in reconciling the different aspects of being and grasping them as a unity. A problem arises only if we try to say one part of this unity is more real than another, or more knowable than another. This is how Descartes distorted the problem of knowledge with his mind–body dualism and his false deduction of the *cogito*. Once we say all that I really know is my own existence we have lost how it is the totality of all existence that enables us to be and to know. In truth we cannot remove the aware-ness of the all and know only the subject, as Descartes hypothetically does in his famous experiment. Nor can we remove the awareness of the subject and only be aware of the all. The two spheres are mutual and grant one another, and the unity between them, as Aristotle says, is *ousia*, beingness. A unique property of the human intelligence is that it may apprehend the presence of everything to everything, and not merely of things in an objective or subjective relation to itself.

This is why Aristotle commences with the question of the being-ness or thinghood of things, rather than some other principle, such as matter or one of the elements. And the recognition of the beingness of things is also an act of being, and the perception of the principles of things is also perception of being. Thus a saying comes down the ages 'The truth of things is the things'.[12] This means that the truth is what most belongs to each thing. It is not an abstraction about things, or a representation of them, but their own-most.

For Aristotle this act of being that belongs to every being is the central enquiry into *phusis* or Nature. His question is always 'what does it mean to be?' and this question is taken further in his *Metaphysics*.

This means, of course, that we can think of being absolutely as well as of being in particular, that is, of 'being in itself' and 'this being'. But we have to be very careful that we do not abstract the thought of 'being in itself' from 'this being'. It is by virtue of our innate knowl-edge of 'being in itself' that we recognise 'this being' and all the modalities of being. It belongs to the intellect to know universals. On this, again, Aristotle and Plato concur. It belongs to the senses to know particulars, and it belongs to the reason to distinguish between universals and particulars.

12 Aquinas says that '. . . truth or the true has been defined in three ways. First of all, it is defined according to that which precedes truth and is the basis of truth. This is why Augustine writes: "The true is that which is"; and Avicenna: "The truth of each thing is a property of the act of being which has been established for it." Still others say: "The true is the undividedness of the act of existence from that which is."' Thomas Aquinas, *Disputed Questions on Truth*, trans. Robert Mulligan (Hackett Publishing, 1994), Volume I p. 6.

Nevertheless, there remains the question of what is eternal, fully actual and good. Is there that which abides fully in its truth and actuality, which is so fully existent that it has no change? What is Aristotle's reply to this question?

His reply lies in the teleology of things towards perfection, towards the fullest possible being. Every creature strives for this fullness of being according to its own form and according to its part in the whole cosmos. Human nature likewise strives for the fullest perfection, and this for Aristotle means the perfection of virtue and intellectual contemplation. These acts alone bring about human happiness. In this yearning of all things for perfection they seek what is beyond their mortal nature of coming to be and passing away. In short, everything in Nature is oriented towards the Divine perfection, and everything has in itself a love of that Divine perfection. This Eros in everything is at once its unifying principle and the power that makes it yearn for the fullest being or actuality. For the human mind it is the yearning for the contemplation of truth in itself. And so for Aristotle God is the act of truth knowing truth, truth in self-contemplation. God and knowledge are the same. Let me conclude by quoting a small section from Book 10, Chapter 7 of Aristotle's *Nicomachean Ethics*:

> But if happiness is being-at-work (*hexis*) in accord with virtue, it is reasonable that it would be in accord with the most powerful virtue, and this would belong to the best part. Now whether this is intellect or some other part that seems by nature to rule and lead and to have a conception about things that are beautiful and divine, and to be either divine itself or the most divine of the things in us, the being-at-work of this part in accord with its proper virtue would be complete happiness. That this way of being-at-work is contemplative has been said. And this would seem to be in agreement with the things said before and with the truth. For this way of being-at-work is the most powerful (since the intellect is the most powerful of the things in us, and the things with which the intellect is concerned are the most powerful of the things that can be known); it is also the most continuous, for we

are more able to contemplate continuously than to act in any way whatever.

. . . But such a life would be greater than what accords with a human being, for it is not insofar as one is a human being that he will live in this way, but insofar as something divine is present in him, and to the extent that this surpasses the compound being [or changeability] to that extent the being-at-work of it surpasses that which results from the rest of virtue. So if the intellect is something divine as compared with a human being, the life that is in accord with the intellect is divine as compared with a human life. But one should not follow those who advise us to think human thoughts, since we are human, and mortal thoughts, since we are mortal, but as far as possible one ought to be immortal and to do the things with a view towards living in accord with the most powerful thing in oneself, for even if it is small in bulk, it rises much above everything else in power and worth. . . . and so, for a human being, this is the life in accord with the intellect, if that most of all is a human being. Therefore this life also is the happiest.[13]

Aristotle holds, then, that the life that accords most with human nature is at once the life that accords with the divine. In this passage we find no dualistic relation between human nature and the divine, and certainly no object called God standing outside things as an entity. Nor does Aristotle reduce human nature to a cause in God. He simply calls 'divine' that which surpasses all change or contraries, and this is intellect, and there seems no necessary distinction between human intellect and intellect as such, or the proper object of intellect which is to contemplate the truth.

So, in considering the ancient philosophical view of nature we find an essential unity between that which is immediately in being and the eternal actuality, truth or good. Nature herself presents herself metaphysically immediately, and not as mere mechanisms to be explained

13 Aristotle's *Nicomachean Ethics*, Book 10, Chapter 7, trans. Joe Sachs, pp. 91–93.

through representations that have no ground in the being or presence of things.

This view, which wholly grants to things the full dignity of being and belonging to themselves, lays the foundation for the understanding of the universe as revelation or divine disclosure, which is the theme of the next essay.

3

Creation and Revelation

~

WE COME NOW TO THE THEME of creation and revelation, and so arrive at a borderline between metaphysics and theology, or philosophy and religion, and thus into the Christian understanding of Nature and the cosmos. This also brings us to the realm of symbol and metaphor, allegory and veiled meaning, and ultimately to the question of the nature of the relationship between God and the cosmos.

From the time of the Church Fathers until the Renaissance this borderline between the visible creation and divine revelation takes on various forms, often contradictory with one another. Nevertheless the various forms really have only two distinct origins. On one side there is the rich tradition of allegorical interpretation of Scripture, which sees the literal sense as signifying a spiritual sense, and on the other side the Platonic metaphysical tradition, which sees the cosmos in terms of the Ideas or Ideal Forms and as theophanic emanation. The Church Fathers such as Origen and Clement of Alexandria, the earliest proponents of the allegorical interpretation of Scripture, each tried to bring these two strands together. But this has never quite held, perhaps partly because the allegorical way of thinking and the metaphysical are really quite distinct modes of understanding, and individuals temperamentally will tend to either one or the other, but rarely encompass both comfortably.

At the heart of the difficulty here lies the question of whether a higher meaning in things *displaces* the things themselves. For example, if the realm of nature is looked upon allegorically, what does this mean to the things seen in this 'other' way? If the Sun, for instance, is seen as a symbol of God, does this symbolic meaning discard the Sun as the Sun, or does it reveal something further about the Sun in itself?

This really is an important kind of question, and it is the reason why Plato in the *Republic* suggests that the young should not read Homer or Hesiod, because they would not understand the distinction between the literal and allegorical meaning.

Once we regard the realm of nature as having a double aspect we run into these questions. We find the same kind of problem when we consider the distinction between particulars and universals. Martin Heidegger has brought this home to us powerfully in his philosophical meditations on the question of being-as-such and beings each in themselves. In the Middle Ages these kinds of distinctions were given a great deal of thought. For example, the distinction between Humanity and each human being. Is Humanity a 'real being' or only a generalised idea? For Aquinas the capacity of the individual to participate in the universal humanity was to be fully human, while for the Nominalists, later on, all such universals were regarded as intellectual abstractions while only particular entities had real existence. But there has also been an opposite tendency, especially found in some Neo-Platonic thinking, in which only the universals are regarded as 'real' and particulars as mere images or shadows of the real. A modern variant of this is the notion that tracing the causal origins of things explains their meaning, so causality comes to be regarded as more real or more truthful than the things themselves.

So the double aspect of things inevitably raises the difficult question of the 'whatness' of things, or the relation of the actuality of things to their truth. In the previous essays I suggested that we must not allow this double aspect of nature to separate the truth of things from their presence, or from their belonging to themselves. I went along with St Augustine and Aquinas who say 'The truth of things is the things'. If we try to hold to that understanding we will be in the company of the subtlest thinkers of the Middle Ages.

To put all this more sharply, on the consideration of creation and revelation we are compelled to decide between two positions: either the creation is a *manifestation* of the Divine, or it is a *representation or depiction* of the Divine. This means that the universe either presences the Divine in some manner, or that it only indicates or points towards

the Divine in some manner. Both versions may be found in the Middle
Ages, and often there are swings from one version to the other.

The metaphysical reason for this peculiar difficulty lies in the
question of the ontological relation between God and the creation.
We have to be aware that God is not here being crudely thought
about as the efficient cause of the creation, which is how the problem
of the relation of God and creation is generally posed in our times
owing to the reductive, mechanistic way of thinking which sees causes
or origins as the answer to the question of the nature of things. This
includes the intelligent design theory. The metaphysical or theological
question as posed by the pre-modern Christians is much subtler than
this because God is understood not merely as the source of all things
but as the fullest possible actuality. God is *the* wholly actual. Within
God nothing remains to be accomplished, either in being, in knowing
or in willing. There is nothing else besides God in terms of actuality.
This is why God cannot be thought of as a cause in the sense of
having potentiality or any unrealised act. Potentiality lies entirely on
the side of the created. Given these attributes, what remains for
creation? If creation is wholly not-God, then what qualities could it
have? Or again, if creation itself is wholly God, where lies the distinction? Ontologically, then, the two extremes are either absolute dualism,
in which there is no relation in terms of being between God and
creation, or pantheism where God and creation are wholly identical.

If, then, these two positions are both false or inadequate, it means
that the terms in which our thought poses the question are in some
way unequal to the real nature of both God and the creation. Or, to
put that another way, even the metaphysical notions of being, actuality, knowing and willing are at best only analogous or figurative ways
of speaking of God and His act of creation. This, of course, is the
theological position generally adopted in the Middle Ages. But the
reason for the inadequacy of the analogous or figurative does not lie
in the metaphysical terms themselves, but rather in the relation of the
thinker to the thought. That is to say, the thought about God is not
yet wholly thought, nor the thought about being yet fully in being.
And this is because this knowledge, in which thought is wholly

thought, belongs to God, because only in God is anything fully actual. The principle is that truth cannot be thought separately from truth.

So long as the way of thinking remains with knowing and known as in some way separate, there is not yet real knowing. This Platonic perspective is powerfully taken up by John Scottus Eriugena in the ninth century.[1] He held that thought must go beyond sense knowledge and inferential knowledge to essential knowledge. Essential knowledge is the knowledge that belongs to the real relation of the intellect to the truth and being of things. It is therefore obvious that if the human mind is to understand the creation as revelation, then there has to be a corresponding capacity of the mind to know it in this manner.

We saw in the previous essay that for Aristotle the soul is potentially all things, and we see here that Eriugena understands that knowledge involves the union of the knower and the known. The Platonic and the Aristotelian epistemologies are clearly complimentary here, if not quite identical. Eriugena brings in a third element from Christian revelation in which the human soul is understood as being itself an image of God's knowing. He takes the passage in *Genesis* which says man was made in the image of God as meaning that man *is* the image of God, since God in Himself has no image.[2] From this he understands the soul as having three kinds of motion. These types of motion are essentially the modes of being of the soul as such, or as Eriugena puts it, 'for the essential being of the soul is not other than its being moved substantially'.[3] He means by this that the motion of the soul belongs to itself as its own nature and is not derived from elsewhere. It is first of all self-moving.

The first motion of the soul is a circular motion around the Godhead. This highest motion is its *ousia*, or beingness, and Eriugena describes it as 'a stable motion and a mobile stability'. This first motion

1 See Eriugena *Periphyseon*, trans. John O'Meara (Dumbarton Oaks, 1987) and Dermot Moran, *The Philosophy of John Scottus Eriugena* (Cambridge University Press, 1989).
2 Ibid. Moran p. 97.   3 Ibid. p 140.

* ... but not until he becomes perfect in himself and not in potential.

is 'simple' and it 'surpasses the nature of the soul itself and cannot be interpreted'.[4] It is ineffable, anarchic, boundless and unknowable.

The second motion of the soul is reason (*logos* or *ratio*), which is *born* of the intellect. Eriugena describes it thus:

> The second motion of the soul, then, is the reason, which is understood as a kind of substantial seeing in the mind and a kind of art begotten of it and in it, in which it fore*knows* and pre-*creates* the things which it wishes to make; and therefore it is not unreasonably named its form, for (the intellect) in itself is unknown but begins to become manifest both to itself and to others in its form, which is reason.[5]

Eriugena here is clearly following the tradition of the soul being made in the Image of God and of the Divine Trinity. He further explains:

In potential

> For the human mind begets from itself as a kind of offspring of itself the knowledge by which it knows itself, and the knowledge of itself is equal to itself because it knows itself as a whole, in the likeness of God the Father Who begets from Himself His Son Who is His Wisdom by which He knows Himself, and His Son is equal to Him because He understands Him as a Whole, and is co-essential with the Father because Whom the Father begets He begets from Himself.[6]

The second motion of the soul, then, manifests in its knowing itself, and through this knowledge of itself the reason unites back with the intellect. From this it derives both its reasoning powers and its creative powers. This motion of the soul is called 'straight' because it reasons from effects to causes and from premises to conclusions.

The third motion of the soul, which Eriugena describes as mixed and 'spiral', is the assimilation of the perceptions of the senses from which the reason can discern the divine causes.

4 Ibid. p. 141.   5 Ibid. p. 141.   6 Ibid. p. 142.

These three motions of the soul are at once outward motions, in which the soul moves towards created things, and inward motions, in which the soul recollects itself through understanding or philosophical contemplation, so that the knowing acts of the soul and the understanding of the being of the soul are understood simultaneously.

The parallels which Eriugena draws between the motions of the soul and the Divine Trinity work both ways.

What we may observe here is that these three motions of the soul are three sorts of acts of knowing, and that for Eriugena the 'knowing act' is what brings the soul into being. For him knowledge has precedence over being, or rather that the 'being known' of things is the same as their being. Eriugena is reversing the notion of the precedence of being over knowledge which he knew from Pseudo Dionysius, for whom things are known insofar as they have being. Eriugena is quite clear about this and says 'The intellection of all things is the being of all things'.[7] That the human soul may know in this manner is grounded in its being the Image of God, and that the Son or Word contains all things, and that their act of being in God is God's act of knowing them. Eriugena gives this view great emphasis in his understanding of the Incarnation, in which the *humanity* of Christ is understood to be omniscient in the same way as his divinity, and that the restored human soul is likewise omniscient.

From this it is clear that for Eriugena the knowing of things in the soul cannot be separated from the being of things, since the knowing comes first both in the human mind and in the things themselves. They have being by virtue of being known *in* God through the Son or Word. It is only through what we might call a 'continuous origination' in God's knowing that things remain in being. Nothing is closer to the being of things than God's act of knowing them into being, and this is why thinking of God as a kind of historical cause is metaphysically confused. Meister Eckhart, four hundred years later, in his Commentary on *Genesis* remarks the same thing:

7 Ibid. p. 143

Further, the reason of things is a principle in such a way that it does not have to look to an exterior cause, but looks within to the essence alone. Therefore, the metaphysician who considers the entity of things proves nothing through exterior causes, that is, efficient or final causes. This is the principle, namely the ideal reason, in which God created things without looking to anything outside himself.[8]

Implicit in what Eckhart says here is that things cannot truly be known separately from God. To know them is to know what is within their own essence and this own essence of things is what Eckhart calls the 'ideal reason' in the mind of God's act of creating. Eriugena takes this way of understanding yet further by seeing all created things as the self-manifestation or self-externalisation of God. In his major work, *Periphyseon* or *Division of Nature*, the teacher discusses with his pupil what it means to say that God creates. He proposes a peculiar idea that the Divine Nature both creates and is created, and proceeds to show how this is not ultimately a contradiction. He argues that if it is created, then it can only be created by itself, because there is nothing prior to the Divine Nature that could create it. He continues:

Well, then: is it not in any case creating whether it creates itself or the essences that are created by it? For when it is said that it creates itself the true meaning is nothing else but that it is establishing the natures of things. For the creation of itself, that is, the manifestation of itself in something, is surely that by which all things subsist?[9]

This is the kind of passage in Eriugena that got him accused of pantheism, but that is to wholly misunderstand his meaning. What Eriugena is pointing to here is that the creative activity of God is not secondary to His essence in any way. His rest in His own absolute being and His creative activity are one in Him. This is one of the

---

8 *Meister Eckhart: The Essential Sermons, Commentaries, Treatises and Defence,* trans. E. Colledge & B. McGinn (Paulist Press International, 1981), p. 83.
9 *Periphyseon* 455b.

divine mysteries, that God is at once wholly at rest and wholly in act, and wholly transcendent and created in manifesting Himself as creation. Therefore anything predicated of God cannot be regarded as distinct from His nature in any way whatsoever. Therefore the coming into being of the creation is not in any sense distinct from God. How can this be so? For Eriugena it is so because the created universe is the self-manifestation of God. He describes it in this way:

> Therefore descending first from the superessentiality of His nature, in which He is said not to be, He is created by Himself in the primordial causes and becomes the beginning of all essence, of all life, of all intelligence . . . and thus going forth into all things in order He makes all things and is made in all things, and returns to Himself.[10]

And further, from the point of view of our perceiving the creation he says:

> For everything that is understood and sensed is nothing else but the apparition of what is not apparent, the manifestation of the hidden, the affirmation of the negated, the comprehension of the incomprehensible, [the utterance of the unutterable, the access of the inaccessible,] the understanding of the unintelligible, the body of the bodiless, the essence of the superessential, the form of the formless, the measure of the measureless, the number of the unnumbered, the weight of the weightless, the materialisation of the spiritual, the visibility of the invisible.[11]

In short, the creation is the mystery of God made manifest – which of course is paradoxical since it in no way ceases to be the mystery. When it is claimed that this is pantheism, what such a claim misses is that Eriugena's understanding of cosmogenesis is exactly parallel with Christ's Incarnation. Therefore it is only problematic insofar as the Incarnation itself is problematic. That is to say, that if the Divine and

10 *Periphyseon* III 683A.   11 *Periphyseon* III 633A, 678C.

the human are distinct and yet one nature in Christ, then the uncreated and the created can be distinct and yet one in God.

We can turn the problem around by asking what else other than the Divine Nature could possibly be uncreated and created, invisible and visible, hidden and manifest, negated and affirmed, unutterable and uttered, unintelligible and intelligible, formless and formed, spiritual and material, and so on, all at once? In an extraordinary way Eriugena has not allowed God to be less than He is, nor creation less than it is. While incorporating the Neo-Platonic understanding of the One as being the most real, he has overcome the tendency found in some Neo-Platonists to *negate* the visible by conflating it into the invisible. We need to bear in mind that the Hebrew and Christian traditions do not relegate the created realms to the 'unreal'. On the contrary the creation is understood as part of the mystery of God and as the manifestation of His wisdom and glory. For Eriugena it is theophanic. Whatever comes into being is at once both itself and the self-manifestation of God. Perhaps the overarching way in which we can grasp this paradoxical mode of creation is through the relation of parts to the whole. Maximus the Confessor, whom Eriugena substantially draws upon, expresses it in this way:

> The cosmos is a unity and is not divided up along with its parts; rather, precisely through its tendency to rise towards its own single and undivided being, it puts limits on the differences of its natural division into parts. So it proves that the parts are always the same as itself, even in their unconfused differentiation; that every whole dwells within every other whole; that all of them fill up the one whole as its parts and are in turn made one and are completely filled in themselves because of the integrity of the whole.[12]

One reason this may sound paradoxical to the modern mind is because we have come to think of the creation as entities located in empty space. But this Newtonian space was not how the ancient

12 Quoted by Hans Urs von Balthasar in *Cosmic Liturgy* (Ignatius Press, 2003), p. 172.

philosophers or theologians thought. Rather, they thought in terms of orders or levels or modes of being, and how these interpenetrated one another. The passage just quoted continues:

> In fact, the whole intellectual world appears as mystery, expressed in meaningful forms through the whole sensible world, to those who are privileged to see it; and the whole sensible world dwells within the whole intellectual world, reduced through the Spirit of wisdom to its basic intelligible meaning. The material, that is, dwells in the intellectual in the mode of intelligible meaning, and the intellectual dwells in the material in the mode of images; but the result of both is a single world.

On this account the sensible or material realm is a manifestation and dwelling of the invisible or intelligible realm, and so the meaning of the material realm exists in the intelligible realm, while the intellectual realm exists in the material realm 'in the mode of images'. Thus the invisible becomes visible, yet in doing so it does not leave the intellectual realm. Nor does it become less through becoming visible. What Maximus wants to emphasise is that the key to the meaning or truth of things lies in the integrity of the whole of reality taken as a unity. The principle of unity is at once the principle that holds all things together as one and as each thing in itself. Indivisible being lies at the root of every particular being, and from this arises the tendency of everything 'to rise towards its own single and undivided being'.

Now, as we mentioned at the outset, various ways of understanding the creation as revealing the Divine emerged during the Middle Ages, and we suggested these may be divided into the metaphysical and the allegorical. Our discussion of Eriugena and Maximus clearly belongs to the metaphysical and shows us the basis of the intelligible, and therefore of the theophanic view, that understands everything to be a self-manifestation of God. The allegorical view does not really deny this, but it assumes that the created world is in some way a *veil over* the Divine mystery. Through this tendency to regard the visible creation as veiling the mystery of God it does not maintain the strong ontological relation between the sensible and the intellectual that Maximus and Eriugena maintain. This is especially the case with regard to traditional biblical allegory and, by extension, poetic allegory generally.

There are very remarkable examples of the allegorical mode of understanding in the earliest commentary on the Gospel of John by the Christian Gnostic Heracleon.[13] He takes the first miracle of Christ, the turning of water into wine, as the revealing of Christ's nature and mission. Three elements are involved in this, the water, the stone jars into which the water is poured, and the wine into which the water is transformed. According to Heracleon, these three represent the three levels of the knowledge of truth. The lowest level is represented by 'stone', which is the letter of the Law. The middle level is represented by 'water', which is the sustenance given within the Law, as portrayed by Jacob's well and by baptism by water. The highest level is represented by 'wine', which is the spirit of truth that transforms into eternal life. Through this first miracle Jesus shows that he has come to transform the water of Jacob into the water of eternal life, and this is why the disciples are amazed.

ignorance
knowledge
revelation

One of the things that is really remarkable about this passage is that the symbolism, or allegorical sense, of stone, water and wine holds consistently throughout the Gospels. For example, when Jesus asks who will cast the first stone when the woman is taken in adultery, he is asking who will apply the old law, or letter of the law, which kills? The old law condemns both the accused and the accuser. The consistent use of stone, water and wine extends beyond the Gospels and throughout the Old Testament. This kind of allegorical interpretation was practised by the early Christian Gnostics, and many of its elements were taken up by Origen – who is the source of this interpretation by Heracleon which he records in his own commentary on John, the earliest Gospel commentary that has come down to us.

13 See Elaine Pagels, *The Johannine Gospel in Gnostic Exegesis* (Abingdon Press, 1973).

ISBN 1-55540334-4

See also ... a large stone rolled across the entrance to the sepalchure...

In this type of allegorical interpretation each object is understood to signify something other than simply itself, and so these objects become a kind of vocabulary conveying meaning beyond themselves. This is precisely the approach of Emanuel Swedenborg in his massive interpretation of *Genesis*. He observes, for example, that in the first three chapters of *Genesis* there are no man-made objects, only natural objects such as stars, trees, herbs, birds and so on, and that these natural objects form the most ancient spiritual language that men once spoke, so that when they spoke of a river or a cloud they meant and understood both the literal and the spiritual sense. He says that this most ancient language was lost and that *Genesis* moves to historical narrative as a second language that conveys the spiritual sense.

Swedenborg's approach, however, does not really go beyond a double sense of Scripture – the literal and the spiritual, or what he terms 'correspondences'. From the early Church Fathers to the end of the Middle Ages four senses of Scripture were normally understood: the literal or historical, the allegorical, the moral, and the mystical. These four senses may be seen to correspond with the hierarchical order of the universe, and it is only because the creation itself has different orders or levels of reality that the Scriptures also have these different levels of meaning. It is therefore perhaps understandable that when the hierarchical understanding of the cosmos was lost during the upheavals of the Church during the fifteenth and sixteenth centuries, the traditional allegorical reading of the Scriptures was also largely lost. The understanding of the cosmos as disclosing or signifying is clearly linked with the mode of understanding of Scripture as allegorical. Nevertheless, throughout Christian history the allegorical approach to the Scriptures had been challenged, often only on the basis that the Christian revelation was for all mankind and not merely for the learned, and therefore its meaning must be simple and single, while multiple Scriptural senses could only create confusion. But that argument is not really a spiritual one and it never prevailed until our modern age where literalist fundamentalism and reductive materialism tend to complement one another and go hand in hand. This has led to historical criticism becoming the dominant mode of biblical scholarship, imitating, so far as it can, the scientific method.

What this simultaneous loss of both the allegorical tradition of understanding Scripture and the hierarchical understanding of the creation shows is that the way in which the cosmos is conceived in any age is bound up with how reality as such is conceived, including, and perhaps especially, the religious understanding.[14]

For those interested in the poetic vision of reality this double loss is surely of great significance. We see how, at the close of the medieval age, the allegorical tradition gradually became merely mechanical before it finally vanished from western consciousness. In this respect *The Pilgrim's Progress* of Bunyan is a good example, where allegory is reduced to mere personification. And parallel with this loss was the rise of occultism, the deliberate *veiling* of meaning in figures and symbols, so that no real relation any longer existed between the symbol and the reality it was meant to represent. It seems to me that it is highly significant that Shakespeare gradually abandons the use of traditional allegorical figures in his plays. These figures no longer had the power to move the soul, and so Shakespeare moves towards more direct correspondences between the inner lives of his characters and the cosmic order of the visible world. He does this through a recovery of the depth and power of the word rather than with the image or the symbol or even the concept.

What Shakespeare does through the word that reconnects with the ancient tradition is reveal anew the correspondence between the inner life of the soul and the order of Nature. The journeys his characters take through the unfolding of the drama always involve a transformation of perception of the world, either by way of a tragic loss or defiance of such perception, as in the tragedies, or through a realisation of the divine order of Nature, as in the comedies. It is because the plays are essentially about the way the protagonists

14 For a thorough study of the allegorical tradition see *Medieval Exegesis: The Four Senses of Scripture*, Volume 1, by Henri de Lubac (William. B. Eerdmans Publishing Company, 1998).

perceive the world and respond to it that modern psychological interpretations miss the mark. Shakespeare's plays are about the relation between human nature and the universal order. All his characters are in one way or another challenged in how they perceive the world, and therefore challenged to bring about a correspondence between their inner being and the universal order. In this regard the plays of Shakespeare are a return to the ancient cosmology of the great Stoics such as Cicero or Marcus Aurelius, for whom the whole meaning of human existence lay in bringing about a harmony of action and being through the contemplation of the eternal order of the heavens. On this understanding of the proper human life the Greek philosophers, the Roman Stoics and the great Christian theologians are all agreed. The human soul is brought to itself through the contemplation of divine presence manifest in the universe. Here the philosopher, the poet and the mystic all meet.

There remains a question not yet touched upon in all we have said so far: given that the universe reveals the Divine Nature to man, what does it mean to the universe for it to be known by man? This raises questions concerning the destiny of the universe and eschatology. We shall explore these themes in the final essay.

4

The Mystical Destiny of the Universe

~

AT THE CLOSE OF THE PREVIOUS ESSAY we asked: given that the universe reveals the Divine Nature to man, what does it mean to the universe for it to be known by man?

From the perspective of the prevailing reductive materialism it is a matter of indifference to the universe whether it is known or not known. Even if things have remarkable order and qualities, and even if the universe is comprehensible to human intelligence, it means nothing in any modern theory of knowledge to those things to be known as what they are, or that they have come to be known. For reductive materialism 'knowing' matters only to the knower, not to the known. From a utilitarian perspective, as with modern technology, knowing things matters only insofar as knowledge brings mastery or control over things, sets them at human disposal. But even if we raise our vision higher and ask it in relation to the pure sciences, the answer remains the same: knowing matters only to the knower.

This question exposes a curious state of affairs. To say it is a matter of indifference to things to be known runs entirely counter to our intuitive sense. When anyone sees the first daffodil of spring its extraordinary presence always comes as a surprise, and some kind of acknowledgement passes between the observer and the daffodil. This happens spontaneously, before one has a chance to present thoughts to oneself about it. Somehow, you and the daffodil being there together in that moment has a kind of sanctity that your being and its being acknowledge. Nevertheless, there is no current philosophical way of articulating this kind of event. It is left to the poets who, as Heidegger remarks, are 'tolerated' but not listened to in our technological age, to acknowledge the mutual or reciprocal presence of things.[1] And the poets do say it, as for example Rilke:

> Could it not be that we
> Are here to say: house,
> Bridge, cistern, gate,
> Pitcher, flowering tree,
> Window – or at most:
> Monolith . . . skyscraper?
> But to say them in a way
> they, themselves, never
> knew themselves to be?
> (Rilke: *Ninth Duino Elegy*)

Here is a way of describing the human calling within the totality of things – to see and to speak the names of things. If man were not here to speak the names of things they would somehow remain in a dark oblivion, and nothing would reflectively know that it was. It is very important that Rilke emphasises the *saying* of the names of things. This is more than merely cognising them or labelling them. To say is to respond, to grant, to bear witness. And in order to speak and to say the human being has to be physiologically formed by Nature for the act of speaking and saying. Although it is often said that man is the rational being, Aristotle in the *Politics* distinguishes man as having language, and it is as the speaking being that he forms his essential relationships with the world, as well as how he forms society.[2]

Is it not curious that modern philosophy has practically nothing to say about man's conscious relation with the intelligibility of things, of the relation of mind and reality? And where there are obvious instances of a conscious reciprocity between the human intelligence and Nature, for example in the mystical sense of unity many people have glimpsed, such instances are either discounted or explained

1 See Martin Heidegger *Poetry, Language, Thought* trans. Albert Hofstadter (Harper Perennial, 1971).
2 Aristotle, *Politics*, Book I, 1253a.

away through material reductionism of some sort. It *is* curious, yet hardly to be wondered at when there are philosophers who hold that any kind of 'mental actions' have no reality. Stuart Hampshire, for example, in his *Thought and Action*, declares that thoughts 'are not part of 'the only solid and substantial world that there is''.[3] Behaviourism and much sociology is based on the assumption that only manifest physical objects, external forms or actions, may be accounted as 'realities'. The reason for this is the prevailing idea that only measurable phenomena count as actual. These are the kinds of reasons why there is presently no generally acknowledged philosophical way of speaking of the relation of mind and the intelligibility of things. The only scientific theory, though contentious, that finds a real relation between the universe and mind is the anthropic principle. This theory claims that the whole structure of the cosmos is required in order to give rise to the human intelligence. It is the only substantial modern theory that has resonances with the ancient Greek philosophers, or which understands the cosmic unfolding as teleologically unified.

In the previous essays it was clear from our explorations of Plato, Aristotle and Eriugena that this modern divorce between mind and the intelligibility or being of things did not exist. On the contrary, the various epistemologies of the ancient world, despite particular differences of approach, all take it as given that there is an essential ontological relation between mind and reality as such, between knowing and the things known. The *knowing act* is an event that both knower and known equally partake in. We also saw in our previous lectures that man is the being who inhabits the creation as the one that reflects upon the truth of things. For Plato and Aristotle this indicates that the proper human life, the life that fully accords with human nature, is the life of contemplation. This is taken up with refreshed vigour with the rise of Christianity, where the aim of the soul is mystical communion with God in all things.

3 Quoted by Mary Midgley in *Heart and Mind* (Harvester Press, 1981), p. 78.

Yet with Christianity there also comes something entirely new. In the Neo-Platonism of the early Christian era the aim of contemplation was to rise to the eternal reality beyond the temporal realms, and this introduced a kind of irreconcilable conflict between the temporal and the eternal. This conflict takes extreme form in some versions of Gnosticism. For example, one form of Gnosticism held that the creation of the world was the evil work of the demiurge who had usurped the divine power and imprisoned the pneumatic souls of the higher human beings in the material realm. For these Gnostics Christ came to rescue those pneumatic souls from the material realm and return them to the Pleroma, the realm of the elect, from whence they had been driven through deception. This doctrine led to the idea that those who believed themselves to be the pneumatics could do no wrong while still in the realm of evil matter, the creation, and so they practised extreme moral licentiousness. To be fair to the Neo-Platonists, it is these Gnostics that Plotinus severely criticises in *Ennead* II, ix.

This form of Gnostic dualism is really quite false to the spirit of the emerging Christianity, and the reason for this is that the Incarnation was not for the sake of rescuing an elect from an evil creation, rather it was for the transformation of the cosmos, so that at the end of time God should become 'all in all' as St Paul says in *Corinthians* 15:27. This all-embracing mystical destiny of the universe has slipped into the background of Christian theology, yet it was prominent in the early Church. One reason for this has been the neglect of what may be called the third aspect of Christ. Great emphasis has been given to the union of the divinity and humanity of Christ, but little to the universal or cosmic aspect of Christ.

In order to respond to our question I would like to take three themes from Christian theology in turn. First, the cosmic Christology as we find it in Origen; second, the anthropology of Eriugena; and third, an aspect of the epistemology of Thomas Aquinas. The links between these will emerge as we proceed.

Origen, the first to write detailed commentaries on books of the New Testament, gives a great deal of attention to the nature of Christ.

His major concern is the relation of Christ to the cosmos. Commenting on *Revelation* 22:13 where Christ is described as the Alpha and the Omega, he writes:

> God the Logos is the Alpha, the beginning and cause of all things, the one who is first not in time but in honour . . . To him glory and honour are offered. Let it be said that, since he provides an end for the things created from him, he is the Omega at the consummation of the ages. He is first and then he is last, not in relation to time, but because he provides a beginning and an end. Here are understood the extremities of the letters, which are the beginning and the end and include the others in between.[4]

The Logos spoken of here is Christ, the second Person of the Trinity. Christ is not only the beginning and the end, but all that is in between, and this means that Christ is present throughout the creation, is coextensive with the entire universe, and may be seen according to the aspects of creation He manifests in. He is at once the invisible and the visible, and His appearance as the cosmic Christ is in no way different to His appearance as the human Christ.

It is clear that for Origen Christ is the aspect of God that appears throughout the universe, and that the historical Incarnation was in a certain sense a *disclosing* of what was always so, just as the New Testament is a disclosing of what was veiled in the Old Testament. Scholars have noted certain similarities with the Stoic understanding of divinity being present in the material universe, but Christ is not identical with the cosmos as the divinity is in Stoicism. Rather Christ is the one *through whom* all things come into being and have their ultimate end in union with God. For Origen the Church, the *ecclesia*, is itself the 'small cosmos' of Christ, in whom are gathered as one family all who have embraced the cosmic Christ as the 'living presence' of divinity. Thus the Church is not merely a human

4 J. A. Lyons, *The Cosmic Christ in Origen and Teilhard de Chardin* (Oxford University Press, 1982), p. 130.

institution, but the mystical body of Christ in whom each human soul is a member. Or, in another symbolic sense, the Church is the Bride of Christ. As Origen puts it: 'And he [the father] who at the beginning created him "Who is in the form of God" according to the image, made him male and the Church female and to both granted oneness according to the image'.[5]

The Church on earth is called by Origen 'the cosmos of the cosmos', while Christ Himself is the cosmos of the Church.[6]

That Christ appears in various forms is in part according to His manner of revealing Himself but also in part according to the perception of the seer. Origen remarks how in the Gospels where Christ is fully visible different people see Him according to their spiritual capacities. Some see only Jesus the son of a carpenter, others see a prophet, but few see the Christ, such as the woman of Samaria at the well of Jacob. Yet while He appears as Jesus in the flesh, He is at the same time in His spirit present everywhere throughout the cosmos.[7] But Christ also may change His appearance to reveal different aspects of Himself, as for example at the Transfiguration which terrified the disciples, or at the Resurrection where only certain disciples were able to perceive Him or recognise Him.

Christ's presence in the cosmos has a double aspect. On the one hand He comes in order to draw all creation back to its original state, while on the other He comes specifically to enlighten rational creatures. As the Origen scholar James Lyons says:

Christ's saving work is an enlightenment of rational beings which enables them to perceive the object of vision proper to their minds and to become divinely reasonable, so that they do all for the glory of God. Their enlightenment is a manifestation of Christ's relationship with the created cosmos. Not only does it result from their participation in Christ the Logos, who as the source of reason is the leading and essential element in their world. It also follows

5 Ibid. p. 137.   6 Ibid. p. 142.   7 Ibid. p. 138.

from Christ's operation, in and through the Church, of constituting the cosmos an ordered totality.[8]

Note here again the cosmic aspect of the Church. As Lyons remarks, it is 'much more than the terrestrial assembly of Christ's followers'.[9] There is also the heavenly Church, and beyond that as Christ's body, Origen says, it 'is every race of men, perhaps indeed the totality of all creation'.[10] And as the body of Christ it is also the 'internal regulative principle of the cosmos'.[11]

All this is far from the general modern idea of the Church, where the mystical dimension of human community seems to be wholly forgotten. It is worth pondering, therefore, what kind of 'institution' could represent the cosmic community of man and all creation. We do not usually think of institutions or communities as having a mystical dimension. Nor do we normally think of the cosmos as having a mystical dimension. Yet this is precisely what the Incarnation reveals as Origen understands it, and what is clearly meant so often in the Scriptures.

The double work of the cosmic Christ – that of drawing creation back to its original state, and that of enlightening rational creatures – takes on very rich implications in Eriugena's understanding of the return of all things to God. It is here that human nature has a special place within Nature as a whole. Previously we saw how for Eriugena the 'knowledge' of things preceded their 'being'. We saw also how for Aristotle the mind is potentially all things. Eriugena adds another dimension to this in his understanding of human nature made in the Divine Image. Human nature, as a creature, stands in relation to the rest of Nature as secondary creator, as the created image after which the cosmos is made. To understand this we need first of all to remember that all things first have their existence in the Son or Word. Eriugena says:

... the Forerunner. John the Baptist

8 Ibid. p. 142.   9 Ibid. p. 142.   10 Ibid. p. 142.   11 Ibid. p. 143.

And then the Christ.

Every creature, then, exists and lives in the Word, Which is the Wisdom of God; and nothing which is in it can perish. For if that which contains, namely Life and Life Eternal, abides and lives without change, then everything which is contained within it of necessity exists, and abides forever, and is eternal life.[12]

Human nature, then, as the Image of God, contains the essences of all creatures in a secondary sense in the intellect. Eriugena describes it in this way:

> MASTER: Does it seem to you that there is a kind of concept in man of all sensible and intelligible things the human mind can understand?
>
> STUDENT: That clearly seems to be true; and indeed the essence of man is understood principally to consist in this: that it has been given him to possess the concept of all things which were either created his equals or which he was instructed to govern. For how could man be given the dominion of things of which he had not the concept?[13]

The dialogue goes on to discuss how Adam is brought before all the creatures in Genesis to see and name them. The Master then continues:

> What is so remarkable then, in the notion of nature, created in the human mind and possessed by it, being the substance of the very things of which it is the notion, just as in the Divine Mind the notion of the whole created Universe is the incommunicable substance of that whole? And just as we may call the notion of all intelligibles and sensibles in the whole of things the substance of those intelligibles and sensibles, so we may also say that the notion of the differences and properties and natural accidents are the differences and the properties and the accidents themselves.

12 *Periphyseon* 908B.   13 Ibid. 768D.

A little later he continues:

> True knowledge of all these is implanted in human nature although
> it is concealed from her that she has it until she is restored to her
> pristine and integral condition, in which with all clarity she will
> understand the magnitude and the beauty of the image that is
> fashioned within her, and will no longer be in ignorance of any-
> thing which is established within for she will be encompassed by
> the divine Light and turned towards God in whom she will enjoy
> the perspicuous vision of all things.[14]

Then after a long elaboration of Boethius's thought he comes to the
fullest implication of his own direction of thought: 'And where else
do you suppose these things subsist but in the notions of them
contained in the soul of the wise? For where they are comprehended,
there they are; and they are nothing other than the understanding of
themselves'.[15]

To understand this rightly we need to keep firmly in mind that
things have their existence through being known into being. This
knowing belongs first to the Son or Word, and in this Divine Knowing all things have their real and eternal existence. Human nature is
an image of this divine knowing. It also must be remembered that
'mind' exists everywhere, even as God exists everywhere as theophany
or self-manifestation. Thus the 'knowledge' that is in things as their
essence, and as belonging to them, also exists in the human mind,
and when understood by the human mind that understanding is also
the self-understanding of the things themselves. Taken in its cosmic
aspect, human nature is the part of created nature which reflects
upon and understands the cosmos, it is the self-reflection of the
universe within itself. But, according to Eriugena, in our fallen state of
forgetting we do not know this. It is only when man begins upon the
return journey back to his beginning that this knowledge is revealed.
And since the return to God involves ultimately an understanding of

14 Ibid. 969C.   15 Ibid. 769D.

all things as they truly are, the return of man also represents the return of the whole universe to God, insofar as the knowledge imparted to the human mind as he was created now also returns to God with man, and the created is united with the uncreated.

In this way the human role in the universe has a meaning for all created things, in this sense as their means of self-understanding and return to their beginning. In attributing these functions to the human mind Eriugena is explicit in repudiating, along with Maximus, the notion of man as the 'microcosm' that some hold. Man is not a kind of duplicate of the cosmos but rather an essential part of Nature as a whole with a unique soteriological function within the whole, and for the sake of the whole. Human nature is the Image of God rather than the image of the cosmos. Yet as the Image of the Creator human nature contains within itself the 'notions' of all things.

With Thomas Aquinas we have a slightly different perspective on the relation of the human mind and the universe, this time, in some respects, perhaps more Aristotelian than Platonic. Aquinas adopts the Greek philosophical notion that all things are oriented towards being known. But for him this derives from his understanding of the relation of the mind of God to the human mind. In the mind of God all things have their true or fully real existence. There they have life and being because they are united with God, and it is only through God's knowing act that they have being. As with Eriugena, for Aquinas God's knowing is the cause of being. All things are known in the mind of God through God's creative act. In this sense, God's knowledge of things is active.

The human mind, as the Image of God, does not know all things through creating them as God does, but rather through receiving them. In this regard, all things that are known into being in God's mind are oriented towards being known in the human mind. 'All that exists, because it exists, is ordered toward a knowing mind, even toward the finite human mind'.[16] We recall that for Aristotle the

16 Josef Pieper in *Living the Truth* (Ignatius Press, 1989), p. 59.

human soul was potentially all things. Aquinas takes up this insight and gives it a higher meaning through Christian revelation. In his *Disputed Questions on Truth* he writes:

> It has been said that the soul is in a certain sense all in all; for its nature is directed towards universal knowledge. In this manner is it possible for the perfection of the entire world to be present in one single being. Consequently, the higher perfection attainable for the soul would be reached when the soul comprehends the entire order of the universe and its principles, according to the philosophers. They therefore see precisely in this the ultimate end of man, which – as we believe – will be realised in the beatific vision; for, as Gregory says, 'what would those not see who see him who sees all?'[17]

Implied in this is that the ultimate end of all human knowing is to know God. For although the human mind *potentially* knows all things, while God *actually* knows all things, since the full knowledge of things resides ultimately in God's act of creative knowing, the human act of receptive knowing can only ultimately be fulfilled in knowing God, from Whom all things have their existence. In this sense the natural desire of the soul to know, and the correlative orientation of all things towards being known, forms a full circle extending to embrace all things in creation and returning them back to their perfect or eternal being in the mind of God.

This double aspect of Divine and human knowing also implies that, although man may do harm to created things in their temporal manifestation, he cannot harm the essence of things in the mind of God. This is because in eternity all things are perfect and immortal, while in time they are vulnerable. This is true for human nature also. Meister Eckhart remarks on the difference between our contingent knowing here and our perfect knowing in the mind of God, where all things are known in their real or eternal nature or truth:

17 Quoted by Pieper in *Living the Truth*, p. 84.

The things we know here as mutable we shall know there as unchanging; we shall apprehend them there in undivided form and close together: for that which here is distant, there is near, for *there* all things are present. That which happened on the first day and that which is to happen on the last day, *is* there all in the present.[18]

From this difference between the temporal and the eternal arises the realm of ethics, which seeks to bring about a true correlation between the eternal order in the mind of God and the created order in the realm of man. From this it follows that man's capacity for universal knowledge, through conforming his mind to the truth of things, is complimented by the practical reason which informs man how to act in accordance with the truth of things. This means, of course, that any unethical act is an act out of accordance with the truth of things, so that knowledge of the true and of the good are ultimately inseparable.

The question of 'the good' opens out the dynamic aspect of things that the mind may come to know. All things that come into existence seek the perfection of their being as their good. Aquinas says '*Good* and *true* and *being* are one and the same thing in reality, but in the mind they are distinguished from each other'.[19] Therefore to see and to know things as they truly are means not only knowing their form or essence, but their manner of being towards perfection or the good. According to the Christian understanding, this dynamic orientation of all things towards perfection is the hidden movement underneath the temporality or transitoriness of things.

Our modern conception of time has been corroded in the same way as has our conception of space, insofar as both are conceived as voids between things. But time seen from a higher vantage point is the proper order of things in their coming to be. From a yet higher vantage point time is the law of Providence distributing to all things

18 Sermon Twenty Five in *Meister Eckhart: Sermons and Treatises*, Volume I, trans. M. O'C. Walshe (Element Books, 1989).

19 Quoted in Josef Pieper, *The Human Wisdom of St. Thomas* (Ignatius Press, 1948), p. 21.

what is appropriate for their true ends within the created order and, ultimately, for their return to God at the end of time. In this respect time may be understood as a form of justice or even of grace.

What have we learned from all this in the light of our original question: given that the universe reveals the Divine Nature to man, what does it mean to the universe for it to be known by man? There is not a simple and clear answer, nor even an answer on just one level.

According to Eriugena it is in a sense through the human mind that things return back to God. For him man has a special function in nature as a whole as the Image of God in which all things may come to self-understanding.

For Aquinas the act of creative knowing in the mind of God that brings all things into being is in a sense mirrored in the human mind into which all things are potentially received. Human knowing acts as a kind of terminus for the outward manifestation of creation, as that towards which all things are oriented. But more than this, through the desire to know created things the mind of man is drawn to know them as they are known in the mind of God, and to know the knower of all things. This beatific vision is the true mystical end of human knowing. In this act of mystical knowing the creation comes into a mystical knowledge of itself.

Origen sees the knowledge of all things as the gathering of the community of knowledge into the mystical body of Christ, the Church. This is worth pondering for a moment since for Eriugena and Aquinas the community of the Church could be taken as given, while for Origen it was still coming into formation. And while it was coming into formation it could be contemplated in its highest mystical sense, as representing the community of understanding that belongs to the whole of mankind. What the early Christians glimpsed was that the only way there could be a universal community of human understanding was at the highest spiritual level, since only at that level do we arrive at what is most essential about human nature and about the truth of the cosmos. Only when things are known in the light of their existence in the mind of God are they truly known, and only through that highest knowing is the real meaning of human community realised. From this perspective we might well wonder what may be possible for humanity to know which can only be known collectively, through the unity of society. Only unity can know unity.

Eriugena and Aquinas are among the few Christian theologians and philosophers of substance who have a vision of how things could be within the creation if man conformed his mind to the truth of things. For Eriugena it would make possible the Paradise that awaits man's return, while for Aquinas it would reveal to man the connection between the eternal law in the mind of God and the natural law that governs the ends of all created things, and which draws them to perfection and to the good.

Do both these visions of things belong to historical time, or are they of things beyond 'this world' as the Gospels often say? Since they involve a transformation of human perception and knowing, this question does not really mean much, unless it means a revision of the meaning of historical time itself. From the mystical perspective, historical time is no longer merely historical time but providential time, and 'this world' is no longer a domain separate from the eternal truth of things in the fullness of their being in the mind of God. The creation is visible to the human mind according to the mode of understanding and self-knowledge that prevails in a civilisation at any given time, while what it truly is in itself and what it truly signifies is known only in the mind of God.

Nevertheless we can at least agree with Aquinas when he says that the ultimate perfection of the truth of things is primordially known in the intellect, and it is because of this real ontological and episte- mological connection between the mind and the truth of things that we naturally seek to know the truth, and to affirm and bear witness to it on behalf of and for the sake of the things known. This is what makes us human and is the proper foundation for philosophical and theological anthropology.

Bibliography

Aquinas, Thomas, *Basic Writings of Saint Thomas Aquinas*, Volume 1, translated by Anton Pegis, Hackett Publishing, 1997
—— *Commentary on Aristotle's Metaphysics*, translated by John P. Rowan, Dumb Ox Books, 1995
—— *Disputed Questions on Truth* (*Quaestiones disputatae de veritate*), translated by Robert Mulligan, Hackett Publishing, 1994
Aristotle, *Metaphysics*, translated by Joe Sachs, Green Lion Press, 2002
—— *Nicomachean Ethics*, translated by Joe Sachs, Focus Publishing, 2002
—— *Aristotle's Physics: A Guided Study* translated by Joe Sachs, Rutgers University Press, 2008
von Balthasar, Hans Urs, *Cosmic Liturgy*, Ignatius Press, 2003
Blanchette, Oliva, *The Perfection of the Universe According to Aquinas: A Teleological Cosmology*, Pennsylvania State University Press, 1992
Bonaventure, *De Reductione Artium ad Theologiam*, translated by Sister Emma Therese Healy, The Franciscan Institute, 1951
Brague, Remi, *The Wisdom of the World* translated by Teresa Fagan, University of Chicago Press, 2004
Clarke, W. Norris, *The One and the Many: A Contemporary Thomistic Metaphysics*, Notre Dame Press, 2001
Collingwood, R. G., *The Idea of Nature*, Oxford University Press, 1960
Cooper, John M., *Knowledge, Nature, and the Good: Essays on Ancient Philosophy*, Princeton University Press, 2004
Duhem, Pierre, *Medieval Cosmology*, University of Chicago Press, 1987
Eckhart, Meister, *Meister Eckhart: Sermons and Treatises*, Volume I, translated by M. O'C. Walshe, Element Books, 1989

70 THE MYSTICAL COSMOS

—— *Meister Eckhart: The Essential Sermons, Commentaries, Treatises and Defence*, translated by E. Colledge & B. McGinn, Paulist Press International, 1981

—— *Parisian Questions and Prologues*, translated by Armand Maurer, Pontifical Institute of Medieval Studies, 1974

Eliade, Mircea, *The Sacred and the Profane*, Harcourt Brace Jovanovich, 1959

Ellard, Peter, *The Sacred Cosmos*, University of Scranton Press, 2007

Eriugena, John Scottus, *Periphyseon*, translated by John O'Meara, Dumbarton Oaks, 1987

Heidegger, Martin, 'The Age of the World Picture' in *The Question Concerning Technology and Other Essays*, Harper & Row, 1977

Inwood, Brad, *The Stoics Reader: Selected Writings and Testimonia*, Hackett Publishing, 2008

Kretzman, Norman, *The Metaphysics of Creation: Aquinas's Natural Theology in* Summa contra gentiles II, Clarendon Press, 2011

Lear, Jonathan, *Aristotle: The Desire to Understand*, Cambridge University Press, 1988

Lilley, Keith, *City and Cosmos: The Medieval World in Urban Form*, Reaktion Books, 2009

Lyons, J. A., *The Cosmic Christ in Origen and Teilhard de Chardin*, Oxford University Press, 1982

MacIntyre, Alasdair, *Whose Justice? Which Rationality?*, University of Notre Dame Press, 1988

Midgley, Mary, *Heart and Mind*, Harvester Press, 1981

Moran, Dermot, *The Philosophy of John Scottus Eriugena*, Cambridge University Press, 1989

Pagels, Elaine, *The Johannine Gospel in Gnostic Exegesis*, Abingdon Press, 1973

Pieper, Josef, *Living the Truth*, Ignatius Press, 1989

—— *The Human Wisdom of St. Thomas*, Ignatius Press, 1948

Plato, *Republic*, translated by Allan Bloom, Basic Books, 1991

—— *Timaeus*, translated by Peter Kalkavage, Focus Publishing, 2001

Schindler, David L., *Beyond Mechanism*, editor, University Press of America, 1986

Thunberg, Lars, *Microcosm and Mediator: The Theological Anthropology of Maximus Confessor*, Open Court, 1995

THE TEMENOS ACADEMY

PATRON HRH THE PRINCE OF WALES

An Academy for Education in the light of the Spirit

The Temenos Academy is an educational charity which aims to offer education in philosophy and the arts in the light of the sacred traditions of East and West. The word 'temenos' means 'a sacred precinct'.

Each year the Academy runs up to 100 lectures and seminars, and occasional film screenings and readings. These range from major public events to small study groups. Our activities are mainly based in London and are open to all.

The Academy publishes a journal, the *Temenos Academy Review*, and other publications in the Temenos Academy Papers series. Recordings of many lectures are freely available to listen to via the website. By these means those unable to attend the meetings can have access to the Academy's work.

The Temenos Academy
P.O. Box 203 Ashford
Kent TN25 5ZT
United Kingdom

Tel +1233 813663

www.temenosacademy.org